Doorway to Wonder

DARREN CARTER

Print information available on the last page

Rev. date: 05/10/2019

To order additional copies of this book, contact:
Xlibris
0800-056-3182
www.xlibrispublishing.co.uk
Orders@ Xlibrispublishing.co.uk

Doorway to Wonder

DARREN CARTER

CONTENTS

Star of Heaven

Star of heaven.
You witnessed the Saviours birth on that blessed night.
You shone with a heavenly light.

Wise men from afar,
Followed you.
A bright, living star.
Shepherds gazed at you and were amazed.
They followed the light of your gaze

To a stable where a baby laid.
In a bed of straw.
Where his Mother loved and adored.

Rubber Duck

Rubber duck.
Rubber duck.
Floating around in my bath tub.

You are yellow like the sun.
You bring me so much fun.

Within the bubbles.
I know you are there.
Your bright eyes,
Giving me a happy stare.

You nudge me in the back,
With your rubber beak.
We both find bath time a lovely treat.

Happy Bunny

The happy bunny,
Is so happy.
She runs around the field with her family.

She smells the flowers,
So wild and free.
It's a hot day,
She takes shade under the oak tree.

The happy bunny,
Sees the birds flying high.
She wishes she had wings,
To fly in the beautiful, blue sky.

Being so happy.
Has made the bunny sleepy.
It's time to go home to her bed.
She can rest her sleepy head.

God of Thunder

God of Thunder.
God and warrior.
With your hammer of thunder,
Heading to Valhalla.

Odin your lord.
Valhalla is your reward.
Viking spirits hail your name.
The Valkyries took them without any shame.

Thor,
The power of thunder is yours.
Let the lightning strike.
Let the thunder be heard to night.

My Umbrella

I love my umbrella,
Like no other.
It was a Christmas present from my Mother.

The wind tries to make it fly.
Will I be like Mary Poppins flying in the sky.

"Arabella,
Bring your umbrella.
It is going to rain.
You will never get wet again."

Church Fete

What a lovely day.
The children are outside wanting to play.

The ladies of the village are laying the tables.
The bell ringers are in the church steeple.

The Vicar is out by the church door.
Hoping the weather stays fine.
As he is going to taste some vintage wine.

Mothers talking about the news.
While Jimmy is blowing is nose.

Mr Jones is taking Rover for a walk.
Little girls playing hop scotch,
Over white squares of chalk.

The men are outside the village inn.
Mr Wilkins is supplying the gin.

The tables are laid with food and drink.

Little Sam will eat too much and probably be sick.

The birds singing in the trees.
The sign of Summer,
Nature is pleased.

Everyone is having fun.
The ice cream is melting in the sun.
The children are playing.
The ladies are eating cake.
Some of the men are fishing down by the lake.

Everyone is gathering to listen to the Vicars speech.
He gives the final blessing and everyone leaves.

Hiding Place

It is time to play.
I love this time of day.
We are playing hide and seek.
We always play this game every week.

I could hide under the table.
I could see their legs and feet.
I don't think it is a good place for hide and seek.

Where is the best place?
I know,
I will hide behind the chair near the fireplace.

They looked all over the house for me.
My brother Robert and my sister Emily.

When the game is done.
My sister calls out,
"Where are you Tom?"
It was a good place to be.
They never found me.

King of the Sky

The king of the sky,
Was so sad.
As he was all alone,
In his magical tower built from stone.

But one day a bird flew into his tower.
She sang a song.
Which filled the king with laughter;

The king gave the bird some bread and water.
He loved the bird,
As she brought him the gift of laughter.

The king of the sky was never alone again.
As the bird would come to him in sunshine and in rain.

Earth Mothers

Under the sky of heavenly blue.
Earth Mothers,
Care for natures blooms.
They care for flowers,
From a seed to their beautiful awakening.
They water them with love,
While the sun is rising.

Earth Mothers.
Natures daughters.
They feel the touch of Nature.
They know when to feed the birds of the Creator.

Nature is their home.
Where their happiness lives.
It is as sweet,
As the honey the honey bee gives.

It is a bond which is handed down,
From Mother to daughter.
Nature loves them like no other.

Faces of Doom

In my nightmares,
I see faces of doom.
They cry out to me, from the darkness and gloom.

They frighten me when I dream.
I wake up and scream.

My Mother comes to me,
With love and a smile.
It takes away my nightmares for a while.

My Mother tucks me in and gives me a kiss.
I hope I don't dream this nightmare,
That is my only wish.

My Mother stays with me.
I feel safe and happy.
I know my Mother will always be there.
When my faces of doom suddenly appear.

The Wizard and the Owl

Under the heavens where the God's dwell.
Lies a castle under a magic spell.

A castle of golden light.
Shines like the stars at night.

A wizard and an owl are wise.
They watch over the world with their eyes.

They gaze into the mirror of truth.
They gaze into the crystal ball of destiny.
They both come from the realm of fantasy.

The wizard keeps all the magic books safe in his castle.
As he is wise and his spirit is gentle.
He has always protected these books.
Only those who know magic take a look.

To understand the spells, you read.
You ask the owl to intercede.

The wizard will read the words and translate.

You must be quick,
Before it's too late.

As the words will disappear from sight. They are the words of Light.
Then the book is closed.
No one will see it again.
As its secrets are hidden from the world of men.

Bringer of the Snow

Blow wind blow.
The bringer of the snow.
You are so white,
Like the winter's night.

You cover the land in your veil of white.
Your breath is as cold as the dead of night.

Nature falls under your spell.
You freeze the water in the wishing well.

Your spirit is felt over the land.
Your breeze makes us shiver where we stand.

Never venture where the cold wind blows.
Stay under your covers,
And watch it snow.

Cyclops

There was once a cyclops who was very alone.
He did not have a friend to call his own.

The people kept away.
They never came close.
As when he roared,
This scared them the most.

In this kingdom was a beautiful girl.
She was blind,
But she was very kind.

One day she was at the stream.
She heard the town folk scream.

The ground shook.
She heard his roar.
This made the girl,
Want to know him more.

"Who is there?" the beautiful girl asked.

"It is I, the cyclops. I am the last.
I am a lone in this place.
I have such an ugly face."

"Let me touch your face," the girl asked.

The cyclops found a friend at last.

The cyclops knelt down.
The girl touched his face.
But she read his heart.
It was full of grace.

They became friends from that day onwards.
It would last forever afterwards.

Goddess of the Moon

Goddess of the moon,
Why do you cry.
You ride your golden chariot across the night sky.

Forever alone.
Forever looking for love.
You look to the moon,
To bring you a heart to love.

Forever searching,
For a perfect love, so true.
You find it in the love of the moon.

The Painting

I sit in my comfortable chair,
And beside me is my glass of wine.
A thought came into my mind.

I gaze at the painting hanging on the wall.
I wish, I wish,
I was part of this world.

The artist created this vision.
A landscape captured without man's intrusion.

A lonely world of green.
Rocks and mountains so magnificent and serene.

The sky of heaven, so free,
And full of perfection.
This is truly Gods creation.

The stream so crystal clear.
I wish I was here.

I lose myself in the painting.
I imagine myself in the fields walking.

Then suddenly,
The doorbell rings.
It brings me back from my imaginings.

Poppy Socks

I am poppy socks.
I wear rainbow socks.
I play with my dolls,
As I eat my chocolate Minstrels.

I enjoy drawing pictures with my coloured chalk.
Last night I had a dream,
I went out for a walk and came across a giant beanstalk.

I climbed the beanstalk and came across a palace of splendour.
I saw a beautiful Princess in a tower.

I invited her home for tea.
She was very happy.

We played with my Wendy House in my bedroom.
She told me she danced in a ballroom.

Now we are together.
She will be my friend forever.

Halo

Only heaven knows,
My dear halo.
I need to know.
Am I a saint or an angel?

Halo,
Are you there?

Halo,
I need to know.
When it's my time to go.
You came to me from the Light.
I dream of you at night.

Halo,
This is the moment,
I've been waiting for.
I will fly with the angels to heaven's door.

Stepping Stones

The stepping stones,
Lead me to a valley of happiness.
They lead me away from a world of sadness.

Across the stream.
I begin to dream.
Of what wonders I will see.
What adventures will be.

Wanting to stay.
The stepping stones will always show you the way.
The stepping stones of hope.
Leading me to a place of love.

Seeing trees ahead.
They look very old.
They welcome a new visitor to the fold.

What I see is a secret.
It's for me not to tell.
It's a beautiful fairy tale.

Tree House

You are whatever my imagination wishes.
From here I can see my Father trimming the bushes.

I could get a telescope and gaze at the stars.
I will be a Stargazer,
Gazing upon a shooting star.

My tree house can be anything.
It brings me happiness beyond everything.

Night Owls

When our Mother switches off the light.
We go under our duvets out of sight.

We switch on our torches under the covers,
And open our comics of adventures.

Where will our adventures take us tonight?
To far of worlds of delight.

Black Knight

Black Knight,
On a steed of black.
Ride on into the night.

Let the mystery reveal.
You lived for the touch of the steal.
The heat of battle.
A war to win.
You did what you did,
For country and king.

A black raven,
On a shield of shining steal.
Makes your enemies fall and kneel.

Your name lives on,
Through the pages of a fairy tale.
Let your good deeds,
Be the only story,
The storyteller will tell.

Snuggle Puss

My fairy godmother came to me.
As I wished her to take away my misery.

From my clothes,
She made Snuggle Puss.
A cat with magical eyes and a happy smile.
She ran to me and we played for a while.

My fairy godmother sat on my bed and watched us play.
I loved this day.
It was like my birthday day.

Before she left,
She told me a secret.
That when night appears,
My new friend would disappear.
To bring her back,
All I needed to do was to meow like a cat.

Security Blanket

Soft to the touch.
I cuddled you so much.
When worries came my way,
With you,
You took them all away.

You made everything alright.
You were always there through my sleepless nights.

I ran to you,
Because every day, I need you so much.
I wished for your comfort touch.

Peculiar Peacock

The peculiar peacock,
Thought everything around him was utter poppycock.

He stood out,
Wearing an evening gown.
He would wear it around my town.

But the peculiar peacock didn't care about anything.
As in his world he was perfection in everything.

Temple of Medusa

Medusa hides in the darkness.
Medusa hides in the shadows.
Beware of her eyes.
She can bring a man to his demise.

Her evil will take you over.
You will be turned to stone, forever.

Her end came from one man.
Perseus, a warrior.
He used his shield to see her face.
He used his sword to end her disgrace.

Pegasus

Listen to my heart beat.
I can feel the suns heat.
A horse with beautiful wings.
Let the angels in heaven sing.

I fly on a wing of a lost prayer.
I am taken beyond man's despair.
The celestial skies, is my home.
It is where the God's can be a lone.

Fly with the Angels

Fly with the angels,
In the celestial sky.
Fly upon a wing of a prayer.
They will take you away from life's despair.

They will take you to where your soul was first born.
They will take you to heavens throne.

A place of wonder and heavenly splendour.
To see the Light.
Your soul will take flight.

Hungry Tom

Hungry Tom.
I need food in my tum.
My tummy rumbles inside of me.
It needs food to make it happy.

It knows the time to eat.
It enjoys a chocolate treat.
If I eat too much, I will get fat.
My hungry tummy doesn't care about that.

Mr Invisible

I am Mr Invisible.
I would like to shake your hand.
But you can't see me,
I do understand.

I am getting used to my predicament.
The reason I am like this,
Something went wrong with my experiment.

I like being invisible.
I like being me.
It is now tea time.
I would love a cup of tea.

Early Bird

I'm a worm in the ground.
I have come out to see what's making this beautiful sound.

A bird in a tree.
It's singing a sweet melody.
I love the sound it makes.
Its welcoming the new dawn as it wakes.

It's an early bird.
He's awake before his friends.
I hope the sound he's making will never end.

Family Time

Gathering around the fire,
On a winter's night.
Cuddle close,
Nice and tight.

Under a throw over,
To keep us nice and warm.
I look at the window,
And see the winters storm.

The Christmas tree with its lights.
Makes us remember the Nativity night.
Our presents wrapped with a ribbon.
It is family time,
At the Christmas season.

Being with the family,
Brings love and the Christmas cheer.
As we wait for Santa Claus to appear.

Sugar Love

Give me some sugar love,
Like the love of my Mother.
You have a heart of gold.
You love the young and old.

You are a fountain of love.
You are an angel sent from above.

Happiness of others,
Is always on your mind.
You are one of a kind.

Gremlins at Work

Gremlins at play.
They course much mischief,
Then they runaway.

Nothing works like it did before.
The Gremlins task is to bring it crumbling to the floor.

When the Gremlins succeed.
Mankind is in anguish and on its knees.

Mankind tries to fathom out what went wrong.
The Gremlins laugh and sing their favourite song.

"We are Gremlins,
The bringers of chaos.
When technology fails it's down to us."

Snowballs

Children gather snowballs from the winter snow.
They are all ready for the children to throw.

The girls and boys are having great fun.
They are playing snowballs under the winter sun.

The playground is full of children at play.
The children are so happy this day.

Tears of Sorrow

I cry tears on my pillow.
Praying for a new tomorrow.

I have cried so many tears.
My Mother took away all my fears.

The love of my Mother,
Took my tears away.
Her love has brought me a happier day.

Leave me now,
My tears of sorrow.
As happiness is what I wish to follow.

Dear Diary

On your pages lie the words of love to my sweetheart.
You are the keeper of my heart.

You hold on tight the words,
I write late at night.

My secrets are forever hidden,
On the pages of your book.
Only I have the key to look.

Sweet Dreams

When I sleep,
I dream of you.

A kingdom of gold,
Mountains of stone,
Forest of green and a beautiful queen.

In my world of make believe.
I dream of beauty and a magical destiny.

Where goodness reigns.
Where the sun always shines.
Where happiness is always found.
Where loving angels are heaven bound.

Angel of Love

Tell me where love has gone.
I wish to be loves only one.
The angel of love has gone.
She has returned to her heavenly home.

Heaven is where love was first born.
Love was in the heart of God's only son.

Somewhere in Time

Somewhere in time,
Was where I began.
Through time and space,
I have seen many an alien's face.
Some were friendly,
Others were scary.
Others looked quite funny.

I am a time traveller,
From another world.
I like returning to the planet Earth.

You have such wonderful things.
I do like human beings.
You have learnt a lot from the past.
But some make mistakes which will last.

You are children in my eyes.

You need to realise.
That time is your master.
One generation will witness the final disaster.

But don't worry.
I can see them so happy.
They have travelled the galaxy,
To find a new home.
Where it is,
I will keep it unknown.

May Queen

The May Queen of springtime and of summer.
Mother Nature will always watch over her.
She wears a white gown of purity.
Mother Nature loves her beauty.
On her head sits a crown,
It brings happiness to the town.

In front of the parade,
The May Queen lies.
She takes the parade to where happiness resides.

Smile

A smile pleases the heart.
It fills it with the promise of love.

A smile takes away the pain of hurt.
It heals with a Mothers love.

A smile is a thank you.
A welcome of peace.
It comes without a price.
It only wishes to give.

Ghost Train

The Ghost Train,
Will take me to a darken place.
Where I will see a skeleton's face.

Cob webs on the walls.
Phantoms flying to the ends of the world.
Fear around every corner,
I am so scared,
I hold on to my Father.

A ghost appears,
It is as white as snow.
A mummy moans
Its words only heaven knows.
Witches casting spells,
Black cats will never tell.

Then the door opens.
I see the light of day.
My Mother smiles to me and all my fears fade away.

Angels Apprentice

I've been sent to earth to gain my wings.
I wish to be an angel.
I wish to fly upon the wind.

I need to do good.
I need to take away your sadness.
I am the giver of happiness.

To do good works,
Day and night.
I will be as bright as the eternal light.

To be an angel with golden wings,
is a dream I've had since my beginnings.

Lighthouse

The sea was angry this night.
But we had the lighthouse,
With its saving light.

It steered our ship,
Away from the jagged rocks.
Without it's light we would have been lost.

Lighthouse,
You are always there for us.
At night,
You are there.
You are our saving prayer.

Without you, the sea would claim many a victim.
But you are our guardian angel,
You have a great mission.

Toy Shop

There's a toy shop in my town.
Owned by an old man in his dressing gown.
With his slippers on his feet,
He begins work on the children's treat.

At night by candle light.
He is busy at work.
Making new toys,
For the children's world.

When the children see his creations.
They open the door to their imaginations.

With their eyes full of joy and wonder.
They will buy one,
Then buy another.

Tears

The heart knows tears well.
It only wishes for happiness by the wishing well.

Tears from your eyes.
Hold the memory of sadness.
When your Mother wipes them away.
Her love brings you so much happiness.

Halloween

A grave yard on consecrated ground.
Where long, lost souls are found.

Throughout the year,
Long, lost souls are in eternal sleep.
The Grim Reaper only reaps.

When Halloween comes with its horror.
These long, lost souls wake from their eternal slumber.

Halloween has come this night.
All the witches take flight.
Ghost are, haunting.
While the children are trick and treating.

Pumpkins mark this season of the year.
It is time for us to have fear.

Red Sky

I look towards the red sky at night.
My loving soul take flight.

I look towards my destiny.
Will I ever find the mystery;

The stars in the heavenly sky,
I wonder why.
What are the stories yet to be told?
Only the secret is known to the young and old.

Rose of Love

How sweet is the rose;
A scent only love knows.

On Valentine's Day.
The beginning of our road to our wedding day.

Each petal,
A cherished memory of our love.
Each dream and word,
The heart felt and loved.

The Magician

The trick of the eye.
The speed of the hand.
The Magician holds up your ten of diamonds.

The Magician is full of magic and wonder.
The children are amazed at his magical power.

Forbidden Hills

Walking in the darkness,
Without a light to show the way.
When you hear a sudden sound,
You will run away.

Lost all hope.
You try to escape the watchers hold.

Watchers in the night.
With their teeth so white.
Their blood shot eyes,
Ready to take a man before the sun rise.

To leave no trace.
Silence falls on your face.
You are lost for words, by what your eyes see.
Is it real or an evil fantasy?

Every night,
Fear will haunt me.
It haunts me still.
What I saw in the forbidden hills.

Watchers in the night.
They bring their fear against the light.

Watch and learn.
Never leave your homes,
When the bell strikes twelve.
Never be by yourself.

Be always in the light.
It will blind the watchers in the night.

Box of Secrets

Excitement fills the air this day.
My box of secrets was hiding away.

To uncover this prize.
Was a pleasure for my eyes.
I have the key to open the lock.
I will be able to take a look inside the box.

What secrets will I find.
A magical gift for mankind.
A super power,
I can use for good.
Or a magic wand made from wood.

The box is open.
A bright light is free.
I will never tell what I see,
As its secret is only for me.

Aphrodite

Aphrodite,
The goddess of love and beauty.
You shower your gifts on mankind.
You are very kind.

From the heavens you came.
A goddess with a beautiful name.

Love never dies, it resides in the heart.
It's for the eyes of the one you love.

Swans in Love

Swans in love.
A perfection of Nature.
But their love is broken,
When Death captures.

There love is so strong.
When one goes to Gods heavenly throne.
The other cries tears, all alone.

No other love can take the emptiness away.
Only death itself,
Can break the chain of misery.

Birds of Paradise

Birds of paradise.
A delight for the eyes.
Rainbow of colours.
They bring to Nature a world of wonders.

In a place of dreams,
So far away.
They look up to the sky and welcome the new day.

Little Fire Lighters

From the heat of the fire.
The fire lighters
are born.

They are smaller than our children.
They skip and run,
As they have a world to burn.

From fire to ash,
They only have one wish.
To set the world alight,
It is their only delight.

King Arthur

A son of victory was born.
Arthur was his name.
A future love would bring him to shame.

With a sword of might.
The Lady of the Lake would take in the night.

He built a kingdom of nobility.
Noble knights,
Sat around a table made from an oak of purity.

Peace came over a pleasant land.
Where noble knights rode with an honourable man.

Into history and a fairy tale of beauty.
He pulled Excalibur from a stone.
Which was his destiny.

Whisper

Speak softly to me my angel.
I can hear your loving words,
So gentle.

You know of loves perfection.
As you love God in heaven.

Whisper to me the secret,
My soul wishes to ask.
Let my love for your Master always last.

Venus and Mars

Our destiny is amongst the stars.
You are my Venus,
I am your Mars.

Let my chariot of love reach your heart.
Let the angels of heaven play their harps.

Living amongst a dream.
Venus your love sings.
The stars are the jewels of night.
They show the world of our love through ages past.

New Dawn

Wait for tomorrow.
A new dawn will follow.
A sun rise will come,
When the whole world will be one.

A new dawn.
A new generation will be born.
They will learn from the mistakes of the past.
Their teachings will forever last.

White Feather

Forever,
As the breeze takes the white feather.
To a place of Nature's wishes.
From a beautiful angel who had the beauty of kisses.

Heaven is so far away.
From those who look for its sanctuary.
You are an angel of forever,
You know of its undying destiny.

Its destiny has the freedom of the white feather,
As the breeze takes it to Mother Nature.

Theatre of Dreams

Theatre of dreams.
Where the world of make believe begins.

This is where fairy tales and children meet.
This is where innocence is so sweet.

This is where stories of destiny are told.
Where children enter the fantasy world.

Take a seat.
You are going to have a treat.
Where your dreams will come true.
Where dreams will always be real for you.

Grim Reaper

The Grim Reaper.
A vision of fear.
Gathering lost souls,
To take to a darken place.
There's no time for saving grace.

You can try to run away.
but the Grim Reaper will find your hideaway.

The Burning Bush

The Burning Bush.
The eternal flame,
A holy fire.
To inspire in Moses the heart of desire.

God spoke through the flames.
Moses listened,
God knew his name.

His faith became strong.
God's belief in him wouldn't be proven wrong.

Moses was reborn.
He walked with his God alone.
Moses lead God's people to freedom. They built a new kingdom.

Candy Girl

Candy girl,
So sugary sweet.
Knowing you is a lovely treat.

In your basket,
Is so much candy.
The thought of it makes all the children so happy.

Monday to Sunday.
Is a candy fun day.
You take all the children's cares away.

You wish the world was made of candy to.
Everyone would love candy as much as you.

Sleepy Land

I wish to enter sleepy land,
Is where I wish to go.
I can dream of walking in the winters snow.
Santa Claus in the sky,
Flying so high.
Unicorns in fields of gold and wizards so wise and old.

The beauty of Nature is seen.
She is the goddess, queen.
All her daughters gather around the waterfall.
They come to the children when they hear them call.

This magical realm of great beauty.
Comes to life when children enter this dream of destiny.

It opens the door to the imagination.
It's a perfect creation.
Whatever you wish,
Will come true.
Dream beautiful dreams,
Sleepy land wishes for you.

Forever, Never Ends

The rising and the fall of destiny.
Brings you closer to heavens beauty.
When your soul reaches heaven,
It will last forever.
As forever, never ends.
You will be with kindred friends.

Broken Arrow of Love

The arrow of love flies.
Across the celestial skies.

Cupids arrow has been broken.
Love has been stolen.
Heartbreak,
Has broken the arrow.
Deep sorrow follows.

Only the power of love,
Can make Cupids arrow one again.
The heart will know of loves true name.

Dove of Heaven

Let the spirit rise.
Let it fly to the skies.
When the night time comes.
Let it rest till the morning chorus sounds.
You are there,
As the dawn begins the new day.
I believe in you, in every way.

The Creeper

Beware of the Creeper.
It's out to get you.
A darken creature of Nature.
Watch out for its wooden finger.

It will take hold of you and never let you go.
It will take you down to the earth below.

A figure cloaked in darkness.
It has no soul.
It knows of no love to make it whole.

Out in the night and pray you never catch its sight.
Your heart and soul to capture.
You will be taken to a darken future.

My Soul needs to Cry

My soul needs to cry,
Holy tears.
God reads the truth of my heart,
Through my sad years.
I feel his love,
In my soul's unrest.
The fiery furnace was my test.

Fiddler's Dance

Under the light of the moon.
The fiddler plays a merry tune.

As he plays,
he taps his foot.
To keep the beat.
For the ladies who love to dance,
find it a treat.

The children hold hands and dance around the bonfire.
You can hear their cheers and laughter.

Everyone is celebrating this night,
Under a sky of delight.

Food of Heaven

Food of heaven,
Feeds the soul.
The heart is full of love and nothing more.

A man in the wilderness.
God gave him food to eat.
A man in rags and walked with bare feet.

Locust and wild honey,
Satisfied his hunger.
Your love filled his soul,
With heavenly honour.

John the Baptist was the voice crying out in Natures wilderness.
He never felt the pain of sadness.

John baptised the sinner with water.
His heavenly love welcomed the Saviour.

Ghost Cry

I came into my bedroom one night.
I saw a ghost crying, it gave me such a fright.
She turned to me from the shadows.
I felt her pain.
Her tears were like the falling rain.

I closed my bedroom door.
To keep her safe from my world.

I sat with her.
I heard her sad story.
I began to cry.
She touched my cheek.
Her fears and sadness were like mine.
We were two of a kind.

Haunted Library

Sitting alone in a haunted library filled with books.
I felt ghost were taking a look.
Looking at me from their hiding place.
I had fear all over my face.

I was told of stories of haunted happenings.
Now I have started seeing things.
Ghost flying about.
Ghost walking in and out.

Every ghost here has a story to tell.
From the darkness I saw ghost from hell.
With their chains of misery.
They made their way towards me.
My legs were frozen to the spot.
I couldn't move.
I couldn't get out.

What I was seeing,
I couldn't believe.
It seemed the ghost didn't want me to leave.

Their faces gave me fear.
I need to get out of here.
Or they will make me one of their own.
I would be as cold as stone.

I heard a noise.
The Librarian was coming.
When the door opened and the light came in.
The ghost disappeared back from whence they came.

"Are you alright?" the Librarian asked from the light.
I couldn't speak a single word.
Because I witnessed ghost from another world.

"Oh! you saw them did you, the ghost?
I see them all the time.
I know each of their names.
You are the last in line."

Morning Star

Morning Star,
From a planet made from love.
Morning Star,
In the heavens above.

When the sun rise appears in front of your eyes,
Morning Star,
Is here for the wise.

Let your red horn sound.
Let it touch heavens crown.
Morning Star,
So bright.
Let your light,
Be my everlasting might.

Lady Marion

Blossom fills the air.
Spring has come.
Lady Marion in her wedding gown.

Her love longed to be touched by a kiss.
Robin came through the mist.
Love at first sight.
The angels sang songs of love so bright.
The rising sun.
The new horizon.
Their love was blessed by heaven.

Sherwood Forest, would be their haven.
A sanctuary Nature truly given.

Nightmare

A nightmare has befriended me.
In the darkness of my dreams.
It lives and wishes to hold me.
Will my Lord set me free!

A stranger chasing.
A danger awakening.
A story yet to be told.
My, darken dream the light of truth to behold.

I wake from my nightmare.
Tears of fear,
Have made their home here.

I call out in the dark,
For my Mother to heal my weeping heart.

My Mother has come.
My nightmare will leave me alone.

Alexander and Bucephalus

Towards the horizon of the sun.
We ride alone.
Together we are one.
Under the might of the storm.

Destiny runs with us,
Like the wind.
It will be with us till our journeys end.

The Gods are with us,
Bucephalus.
We ride into fame and history.
Let our story be loved by the worthy.

Valley of the Kings

Under the desert sun.
A people came as one.
To build a new kingdom out of stone.

The people came with joy in their hearts.
In the desert haze,
They gave their Pharaoh praise.

But time was their enemy.
It took the peoples destiny.

This wonder will be lost,
By the desert sands.
For a new generation to be born,
To find.

Keeper of the Dream

Behold the dream.
By the crystal blue stream.
Under the rainbow of love,
Lives the spirit of a dove.

Heaven came this night,
And a star in the night sky shone so bright.
The birth of a new way was born.
Many will follow this babe to a tomb of stone.

Love is the true way.
The path holds the dream.
For the many to truly believe.

Little Miss Storm Cloud

In the sky,
The storm breaks.
Thunder and lightning shake.

Little Miss Storm Cloud,
So soft and gentle.
She loves to make everything so beautiful.

She loves the rainbow,
In all its colour.
She hides,
When she hears the lightning and thunder.

Nature cherishes her.
Nature looks on her as her little wonder.
Little Miss Storm Cloud,
Who is scared of the lightning and thunder;

The flowers are happy when they sway in the breeze.
As Little Miss Storm Cloud answers their needs.

Her tears of rain,
Will always fall;
She is happy when Mother Cloud calls.

Promise Land

I'm in heaven.
A place I've always believed in.
A beautiful dream.
A place of daydreams.

A promise land,
A gift from God to mankind.
Food for the soul,
Love for the heart.
A place where man can be his better part.

To be in God's presence.
To feel the warmth of His essence.
To a place we shall go,
Across the desert of sorrows.

Teacher's Pet

A teacher's pet,
That's what I am.
I enjoy studying for my exams.

Revision is the key to achieve a perfect A.
Now I got my first one,
I'm away.

I love going to school,
That's what I do.
I love learning in my classroom.

I place a red apple on my teacher's desk.
It is my way of looking on my teacher as the best.

I look forward to a new day.
So, I can go to school,
To learn and play.

Doorway to Wonder

"Come and play,
The sun is out today."

My Mother opens the door,
To a place of wonder.
Where I can play,
Without being in danger.

In this place I can be whatever my heart desires.
A knight battling against a dragon with fire.

I can ride my bicycle around,
Or gaze at Nature from laying on the ground.

My imagination runs wild and free.
It is a wonderland just for me.

St. Francis of Assisi

I reach for heaven,
Where God is hidden.
I open my eyes to see,
the love God has for me.

I love you with a heart full of loves longing.
I can hear the angels calling.

I see Nature all around.
I look on your kingdom on earth as holy ground.

The birds of the air and the animals in the fields.
It makes my soul cry with tears.

God, I gave up my world for yours.
My soul hungers for your words.

Sainthood is my reward.
In this beautiful world.

Office Cat

The cat has got claws.
It's meowing at my door.
If I let her in,
She will put the office in a spin.

Everyone adores her.
She's the office cat.
When you stroke her,
She arches her back.

She will meow for another stroke.
She will want her cream,
That's no joke.

We play with her on the floor and on our desks.
She is well loved.
She is the best.

She loves to play.
We have our work to do today.

Her name is Jessy.

She stops us from being busy.

She sits by the window and watches the world go by.
At the end of our working day,
We stroke her and say goodbye.

Christmas Stockings

The sound of jingle bells ringing.
Santa Claus is coming.
His reindeer pulling his sledge across the sky.
Bringing joy of Christmas to children's eyes.

Christmas Stockings,
Hanging by the fireplace.
Waiting for Santa Claus to show his face.
On this cold night,
He leaves presents to bring children delight.

Long Days of Summer

When I was young,
Every day was an adventure.
My Mother kissed me on my departure.

To venture into the long days of summer.
I only have to remember.

Sharing this time with friends.
Friends to the bitter end.
We went everywhere in these long days of summer.
It was when our friendship became even stronger.

Down the path to the pool.
That's where we all acted like a fool.
Diving into the water so clear.
We were having so much fun,
Time just disappeared.

We stopped for ice cream,
As it was such a hot day of summer.
I remember it melting,
I had to buy another.
My friends thought it was funny,
they joked about it as we carried on our journey.

But these long days of summer had to come to an end.
I said, "goodbye to my friends."

Magpie of Sorrow

Magpie of sorrow,
Please, don't cry.
The Magpie of joy is flying in the sky.

Fly away,
With happiness.
Say goodbye,
To your sadness.
Together as one,
Under Gods holy sun.

Phantoms of the Mist

Phantoms of the mist.
They come by a darken wish.
They appear to the unexpecting stranger.
They are the bringers of danger.

To look at these creatures in the moonlight.
Brings your soul to fright.

Many have been taken.
Man's spirit has been broken.
When they appear,
You freeze with fear.

They take you,
There's no escape.
They take your body and soul,
Before the morning breaks.

Printed in the United States
By Bookmasters